In the Dream You Wore Your Yellow Leaves

In the Dream You Wore Your Yellow Leaves

poems

Sherri Bedingfield

GRAYSON BOOKS
West Hartford, Connecticut
graysonbooks.com

for my father
for my Grandmother Inez
and my two sons, Ken and Reed

Contents

A Scent of Earth

Too much time has passed, and I am lonely for a forest,
a woodsy place with gray stones of any size, smooth or rough.
A scent of earth, brown soil, a damp muddiness after spring rain.

Young pines stand tall in their small elegance, taking the sunlight
before the deciduous trees leaf out and reveal their tufts
of delicate new leaves. These trees are waiting.

No quiet like the quiet of trees standing in their places, roots waking
to fungus, holding their brown-gray bare branches
with tiny red or yellow buds swelling.

A vernal pool mirrors trees and sky. A still green Christmas fern
from last season waits over soft brown pine straw
for spring's warmth to make it stand again.

A scatter of leaves from last October carpets the trails
welcoming walkers. It has been too long. Meet me there.
It can be our first walk.

Seedlings

If the rain is right in the wide field, in the mix of clay
and cotton-white sand packed just enough to coddle them,
the seedlings grow. They spread their tiny tender roots
wide and deep under a sun-baked surface.

We see hundreds of trees, evergreens and deciduous,
loblolly pines, and at the other side of the field, saw-toothed oaks.
My dad's hands planted many of them.

Across the weeded dirt road a cemetery waits under long leaf pines.
In summer leafy oaks fill out the sunny spots. A thicket of wisteria
will bloom along the wire fence in April. Our family tombstones mark
the passing generations. Pine straw blankets the graves.

I follow my father between the neat and narrow rows of young trees.
So many times I have followed him, my first mentor.
Once his six-foot-three frame walked this land in long strides.
He checked his seedlings often, tested the markers at his borders.

A farmer proud of his small spread. Now his shoulders
curve forward, one hip sits higher than the other, scoliosis slows him,
makes his steps shorter, uneven.

We return to the house, the sun directly over us, showing short
    shadow.
We walk through a brood of busy chickens in spots of sand
and swing the screen door wide open.
Mother still in her robe hears us as she watches her soup steam.
With a whisper, the screen door closes slowly behind us.

Mid-February in Georgia

Again, before dark, a chevron of geese flew down from Virginia, or more likely, from the reservoir off route 72. I never tire of seeing them. Some stay here, spend their winters in the south. The flying geese seemed high in the sky as the highest clouds, carried by wind currents. They glide through air like ships over smooth waters, level and focused. Dad, a navy man, would say their long necks extended into air-currents, like bowsprits on a boat- offering less air resistance. I could hear them shout and bark as I stood on my front porch.

At Berkland Park on Tuesday there must have been a hundred of them strolling around the grounds, honking their comments to each other as they crossed the parking-lot black-top to rocky sand around the orange pond reflecting an orange sky. The geese were patient with one another, it seemed to me. Almost two by two, they pushed off the pond's shore, launched themselves to glide through chilly waters. "Look at them! Listen to that racket!" Dad would have said, his pale eyes shining in the moment. Another time he might have said "It's September 2nd, the sun has lowered itself in a clear sky, soon we'll hear the geese". When Dad heard the geese call, he'd go to the closest window or step out the nearest door. I always knew where he was when the geese called. Even now I see his face when I hear geese fly over. I hear him say, "You'll see them, there, see! See them!?"

Reed, the Front Seat

Remember we used to drive around. Sometimes we had a destination, other times not, we just drove. The weather could matter, mostly it didn't. Just the riding, the ride itself, the two of us in the front seat. Roaming the roads, we were free souls. We could talk about anything. I'd get excited at our front seat freedom, our back road adventure, our highway vista. It was just the two of us. You loved to sing and play CDs. Our capacity for chorus was stunning. We would get playful when we didn't know the words. We'd make up lines. I don't remember most of our duets. I remember the joy though.

The Field

for Ken

You stand across from the tall corn.
Such a strong man.
A young man and an old man
together at the same time.
The intensities of nature
sometimes blind you.
Flashes of the eternal come to you.
You stand with the trees and watch
light pour through their branches,
an impression of the Whole.
A vision, a parallel universe.
You, Ken, you're a person of the light.

Westmoor

We've walked to this bench before,
it seems to be our favorite. Long eared Eastern
cottontails gobble clover's white flowers.
Rabbits graze on open paths weaving through
the yellow field. Hefty bunnies,
five feet away from us, nibble calmly.
You love them.

Late in the day, but before dusk,
swallows dart and dive, dancing in the sky
catching their prey. Tops of trees wave with
evening's restless air. Bergamot, wild bee balm,
shows blue flowers next to tall red
hummingbird plants.

There's nothing here that's not beautiful.

We came to know each other here, meeting
between other obligations. Remember
the hawk that flew over us on our first walk?
Its white belly, shrill hawk call, it looked
into my eyes slowly. It looked at you even longer.
You said the hawk blessed us, as only a hawk can do.

The sun slips behind the horizon of hills
and trees. Here we are, still visiting Westmoor
almost fifteen years after we saw that hawk.

Before Snow, December

I sit on the only tall stone in this forest of leafless trees.
Birds call under white afternoon sky, so many I can't
name them or identify their songs. The oldest tree
with the largest trunk holds their feathered menagerie.
But I can't see any birds in detail.

I see you standing as straight as the tree behind you, but you
don't see me. Your face shows a quiet joy. The low grass, yellow
now, waits for a dry breeze in damp air. I think a smile but don't
move my mouth. I am still as a stone. I am stone showing part of
itself but you can't see me. The lilies have died back and their hill
is winter roots and broken branches. I want to leave something.

I could be a mica-chipped stone partly exposed from the cold dry
earth. Or I could walk with winter's slow trees.
I want to leave something.
I keep remembering or forgetting, forgetting or remembering.
You still stand quiet, gazing through the leafless trees.

Elegy for a Black Locust Tree

The canopy of your shade rested over my father
on the backyard chaise in July, as he read a collection
on war ships, writing in his spiral notebook.
    That was your last summer, old tree—

down since October, and it's January. Gone
after thirty years, leaving a desolate gap
in our landscape. I liked how you
    threw afternoon shadow

across our dining table—Compound leaves made
lacy fans of shade with dark summer green.
Your trunk and branches dense as iron, stronger
    than some stones—never blocked the eastern sun,

as if you knew it was Mother's favorite light.
Each day you stood protecting earth's creatures
in your way. After September your long black
    bean seeds flew about the neighborhood.

Over years you separated the porch from its foundation.
Pushed it to an awkward angle we only noticed after
I slipped in an ice storm. That spring we found
    your curious roots moving through cement,

between stones, entering the basement. There was no
stopping you. Before the tree cutters came
I apologized every time I walked past you,
    once, one of the tallest trees on Magnolia Hill.

When you were cut a family came and took your logs
for firewood. One night I dreamed several neighbors

helped me move the house to another part of the yard
   so you could stay.

In the dream you wore your yellow leaves.

Animals Come

On a cold spring morning, a murder of shining crows
did not fly or hop, but strutted along my street.
They walked in the sun, down the blacktop to the end
of pavement to stay off the snow.

In June, driving the back roads after a movie,
I looked for fireflies in evening fields.
There were none till we pulled into the driveway,
where they waited, with night sounds
in the night air and, for a moment, took us out of time.

A Luna moth arrived in the breezeway,
appeared dead, but no,
it hung with its huge eye-marked wings beside the light
sending signals with scent. "Come, come here."
The next day it spread its wings on the north side
of a brick wall, a visual melody.

At the end of summer we traveled a two-lane
road divided by a yellow line, no traffic.
We passed a barred owl, Athena's hunter,
with its catch in the center of the road. It watched
us pass without flinching, without screeches,
never stepped off the painted line, foot and claw clutching rabbit.
No apologies.

Broad-Winged Katydid Calls in September

Acorns and narrow-leafed maple seeds
collect everywhere trees are. Branches swell with seeds
that dive, spin as helicopters do, float like feathers—
twirl, drift, rest briefly under mother trees—

if earth hasn't grounded them at the edge of a half-buried stone,
or tucked a few under thick-bladed grass, they lift, dry as air—
fly and fall again.

Katydid's delicate wings are veined like maple leaves,
its grassy green body like a long new maple seed. Its night calls
are deeper than the cricket's bell-chirp.

All day katydid shelters, invisible, tucked into shrubs
and trees. It eats pointed maple leaves in the dark,
until time for singing.

A night song, it clicks with crispy sounds, a raspy whisper.
A future mate listens with her whole body somewhere
in a haven of darkness.

If you were able to see its face, its tiny red tongue,
quick black eyes, elegant legs; long and stilted,
a whisper for wings—katydid moves as dancer—
its beauty could still you, take your breath.

April's Good Neighbor

I go to the porch and watch
a sweep of muted purple dim
to darkness behind the pines
on Augusta Hill. The scent
of new growth intensifies
as breeze disappears. I hear
a sound before I see the animal,
a soft snort.

A pointy white-faced something
slowly climbs the four steps
of the porch. A possum has come.
Two brown eyes look back
into my eyes. It sniffs the porch
floor, munches scattered bird seed.

Possum finds the dog's water dish,
takes a hearty drink. No water spills
over the sides. Possum has round brown
ears pointed forward, a thick brush
of uneven white and gray fur.
It's an American marsupial.

I know this possum eats more than 5,000 ticks a year.
For that, I call her Good Neighbor.
She's quiet, persistent. Her kind has been around
since the age of the dinosaurs.

I watch as possum discovers vernal pools
in empty pots and drinks. Possum
turns and in the light from the kitchen window,
I see joeys on the mother's other side.
I let this quiet night feeder take its time.
I dim the light slowly.

Lady Slipper

A glimpse of yellow,
a purse,
a bag-of-a-flower
a wild orchid.
Painted with scarlet
brush strokes.
Petals tipped in purple.
Sepal brushed brown
competes with petals.
Almost weightless.
Body like a small child
with yellow boots
exploring the forest
after a gray spring,
New England rain.

Spring, a Dry Season

for my father

Roots, dry-topped, next to fallen branches, brown and gray, left from last season, wait at the edge of a small vernal pool. At springtime this place was once a beautiful lake. A small swampy area was on the north side. Today no skunk cabbage is in its usual low shady places, nothing green yet. But it's still early.

It was early spring when we walked this trail together. It was the last time. You wore your hunter green duck boots. When the lake was here, there were mossy shallows. Turtles sunned on mounds of earth, gray logs, or curled roots. Sunnies, carp and perch lived in the deeper waters. This season banks are dry in many places. Western light that fired water's flat surface, when water was here, slipped to dusk unreflected.

A small cat, feral thin, watched for a catch beside a thicket of scrub oak and Christmas ferns. Its mother abandoned it, you would have said. No sight of turkey. No rabbits or skunks. The sky was almost quiet. I didn't hear crows. If you were here, you would have noticed them missing.

To See the Salmon

I see the salmon at the viewing windows along the fish ladder at Bonneville Lock and Dam on the Columbia River. Grand fish of wisdom and magic, their life cycle, story and myths are posted on the wall across from the large windows. This month, August, they're swimming their return journey from the Pacific to the place of their birth in fresh river water. They're spawning, soon to create new nests. It's a gift to see them as they journey.

Their spotted dorsal fins are silvered, green, or gold-toned. When spawning, female salmon often change color to attract a mate. The male's mouth can take on a hook-like shape. Their sharp teeth on the lower jaw become more prominent. The male protects his mate and the nest area she's prepared. Females arrange stones in a way that cradles their eggs.

Pacific salmon are often called Chinooks, a name inspired by the Chinookan people of the Pacific Northwest. King Salmon have lived in the waters from northern California to Alaska for at least five million years. Chinooks, Pacific salmon, or King Salmon are known as the fish of knowledge. Powerful, historic, huge beauties, the people consider the fish immortal. The salmon are secretly humans disguised as fish that return each spring to feed themselves to the Chinookans. The salmon are sacred. If the temporary people return the bones of the eaten fish to the waters they came from, the humans become grand fish again and continue their lives passing from fresh to salt waters, returning to fresh water to nest.

In the hallway of windows facing the fish ladder, it is surprisingly quiet, considering the crowd of people here. I imagine most people are captivated by the power, strength and story of such stunning creatures. I am. As I gaze at the fish in motion my anxiety evaporates. Watching them offers peace.

African Panorama

Shifting across the yellow
and brown savanna, giants
in their gray skins create
a low thunder.

A journey for water
towards a lake
they can smell
in the distance
under circle moon.

Elephants march.
A clan of mothers
and sisters. Calves trot
between three pairs
of females.
Their protectors.

The sky hesitates, holds quiet.
Jackal buzzards watch
with quick eyes.
They sit motionless.
Giraffes under trees
stop eating.

Shadows move
beside the elephants,
thin images, no longer
what they once were.
Ghosts of elephants past.
Murdered for tusk,
lost at war, sold to circus.

Giraffes watch
as they pass
then refocus on eating.
Gray giants walk
with their kin
until they disappear
in a purple haze of dry dust.

At the Road's Edge

Beside the highway trees cast shade
in late afternoon's slant light.
I slow down—something else
is there—on the ground
a body
a cougar, a bobcat.
I pull off the blacktop
beyond whatever it is.
My rearview mirror shows
a stretch of fur
a tail, arrow straight, short.
A bobcat.

A closer view shows
its face has yellow
markings next to tender brown
and gray. Black outlines
its closed eyes, brown spots
set off white whiskers.
White around its chin and neck
the fur looks clean, soft,
a young cat. Delicate face
like someone's pet, a kitten
but bigger. Then I see the wound,
its displaced shoulder—
crushed ribs—no breath.

Someone was speeding. The bobcat
is gone now, from its woodland home,
its neighbors, from the peepers' song,
from the field where it hunted
under red tails at gloaming.

The deer and turkey won't miss
its silent presence.
Lost now, ghost cat.

After You Left

I didn't think it would
turn out like this—
Wait.

I whisper to the air
as you are already gone
from your red hills,
from your brown office
with reams of paper

from the hallway
you walked every day
many times,
gone from this
small hospital room.

Wait
I shriveled in silence,
reduced, darkened,
pulled back

and you reached past
your ventilator,
touched my face,
your kidneys gone
before you.

Wait
I wanted to open the window
for you to hear the singing
crickets—for you to see
the scarlet oaks
on Walton Avenue.
They are here for you.

Carlene

Walking toward the river, once, I followed a woman. She had dark hair and reminded me of my long-passed cousin. I always wanted her to be my sister.

In yellow grass, by the walk, a flock of grackles chattered and grazed. Someone was fishing at the short river-dock. That day two older women under wide-brimmed sun hats shared a bucket of minnows for bait.

Carlene and I, if we stood side by side, would never look like sisters. Carlene, dark haired with hazel eyes and me, a pale, skinny, blond girl. She, like me, didn't have a sister.

She worked in her husband's office with two other women. Her husband slept with all of them. She never got over that. And there were other things, reasons. She shot herself in their backyard next to a blooming azalea bush.

When I walk, especially in April, I walk with Carlene. I imagine I'll see her at the next corner. At Martha's, the luncheonette on Main Street, we'll get our sandwiches and old-fashioned Coca-Colas.

In Our Bed

My grandmother's bed
a boat for dreams,
its mahogany posts reaching up
to a white laced canopy sky
that hung over us on warm nights.

Tall windows welcomed
a hazy sun for yellow mornings,
opening our days from the east.
She would tell her stories:
her childhood, her nine brothers,
her father a minister,

a man who lost
three wives to early death.
Her stories about stepmothers, their pictures
on her hallway wall, all three of them.
Her uncles whittled and whispered
their secrets on the front porch—

Her eyes would gauze over when she
was sleepy. She talked about Sweet Jesus
on those honey mornings.
She would stand in front of her mirror,
a tall woman—I am like that.
Her gray blond hair full and thick,
hung like a waterfall.

She looked in her box of jewelry to find
round earrings. Each day she wore
her flowered cotton dress,
her tiny ankles bare.

My grandfather had his own room,
I played in a sunny spot with trinkets,
his gifts to me, from the bottom drawer.
After his travels she would lie with him,
in his brown bed and learn the news.
They would talk and talk and talk.

Your Horse

You talked about horses at dinner.
After, in your bed, your grandmother's
bed you'd painted cream, you imagined
your dream horse. Caramel colored, dappled
gray on her rump. She could stand the heat
of a Georgia July. She'd be able to smell
lakes or cool creeks and get you to them.
She'd be beautiful. Beauty is protection,
survival. Her legs would be like steel springs
even after a night of wet frost.
Your horse would look you in the eye
every day.
She would snort and stamp
her hoofs at anyone who turned on you,
notice if you were so lonely
you stayed with some guy you didn't know
from that bar beside the river on Whaley Street.
Your horse would be fast,
lightning fast,
fast as a slap.   Running
with you on her back.   From anywhere.

Addiction, Summer Kiss

Like falling into a lake
     deeper than you ever thought
     lakes could be. Like an immersion.

This love—like a drink of starlight
     or almost drowning,
     you can't tell the difference.

You thought it was a summer kiss,
     but a deceptive needle captured you
     with its sweet venomous bite—
     A room held you in its blue haze—

for weeks or months, a tender time
     you thought, you forgot the way out,
     stayed past time to go.

Aimless and empty
     you paced and pulled for breath.

Not thinking, not remembering, not washing
     your hands or hair. You used to know
     things. Now the skin of your face
     is hard and thin.

After a long time, you're back but different—
     You want to start over—

the memories make you cold like the lake,
make your hands shiver.

Volcano

*May 18, 1980, was the day. Fifty-seven people died, more than 7000
animals were killed and thousands of trees and forest understory
burned. Many believe that Mt. St. Helens will erupt again.*

For years I dreamed of walking the mountain. Following crooked
trails to witness its waterfalls, its craters. Maiden Mountain, home of
Sasquatch. Is the mountain a woman of sacred fire or a mother enraged?

The mountain called me. She said, "Come, come in the stark white
winter or at the end of summer. Just come." I went. I went to her still
swollen base, her belly. I could feel the life in her as my feet touched her
trails, see parts of inner earth turned up and over. Chunks of lava bigger
than I am, rooted like the odd teeth of someone very old, spaced apart
and colored like corn and bark. I tracked a broken path to the newest
crater; an eruption of gas and ash opened a spirit-plume, like the fire
that brought the natives to their knees.

Volcano, the raged mother, I think while walking. And you, a storm
yourself, long gone, take my thoughts again. You, your face darkened,
unable to still for long, brows pulled together, promised me again
and again—and your rage exploded anyway. There must have been
an absence of something or a strange private spark that ignited itself
inside you. It had to burn down to find a quiet and start again. I missed
you, a weightless absence even when you seemed to be present. I'm still
surprised to find you gone. In my dreams you always smiled. Your hair
is thick and twisted in a long braid. Our reflections glisten in store front
windows. I dream of our times with soft edges.

Now on Mt. St. Helens birds graze around skeletal stumps. Thick grasses
grow up through dark dirt and thin ash. People of the mountain, new
and old, settle again. The shop owner's cousin has a rebuilt cabin on a
ridge. Waters of Spirit Lake, dark with their depth, almost clear again,
glisten.

After

At three in the morning
after the election,
I sat up. Even though I
didn't know.   I knew.

I walked outside barefoot
over grass and felt the earth
support the skin on my feet.
After crossing the dark yard.
I stood beside the yew
I planted 25 years ago.

A breeze rattled copper leaves
on the old oak above the yew.
The oak stood here before these
houses were built.

Standing there, in the dark, I hoped
I would finally find a quiet
with the oak and the yew cradling the wind.

Facts About the Body

The eyes   all of our eyes   filled with love
or anger and the other feelings   The eyes
with their wide questions   small answers

And the hands with their   constant motion
moving about   reaching and holding on
helping hurting   or simply fixed still with sleep
hands that hang at our sides   fold in a lap

And the mouth   with its twists   its sticky shiny words
words like   glass or ghosts   words like powder
words   with their heavy weight

And the heart with its sensitivity   with its hum
its even rhythm   beat beat   beat beat   sweet heart
waiting on a sleeve   amazing machine   no thought of safety

My heart   with its whine   its messy wounds
worrisome nature   its stony withdrawal
who knows where it goes
to clear its fear

Women Walking

Sunlight catches folds in their clothes,
going and coming, returning to kitchens,
studios, an office, a lover or a library
after morning tasks, the women walking.

Muses in motion, daughters of Venus
crossing streets, entering buildings,
riding elevators.
Going and coming.

The ambivalent stand and wait
like a riot of pink and yellow tulips
in a sidewalk garden or a box of crayons
spilled on a white counter. Afternoon drifts

toward them all. Some in shaded stalls
to work, hair clipped short or gathered
behind their ears, shoulders squared,
backs straight, focused. Some would sketch

your portrait under leaves or clouds.
Some sell you semiprecious stones,
shoes or silver chains, tomatoes,
beets, or olives.

I sit at the café window
curled over my coffee wondering again
about death. I imagine the rest it might offer,
a sort of prayer.

The passing women return to my view.
I think of Persephone.
how she came back into sunlight
like these women walking.

Dancer in Shifting Light

Outside in the grass
under a shifting light,
a dancer catches your eye.

Moving to a symphony of silence
with serenity. Cloud over cloud
over green, open to blue.
Surely there is bird song.

Who calls her? Elation shows on her
face, in the blur of her hands' moving.
Her eyes close a moment, you see
the corner of her mouth lift, a smile.

Her dress, yellow then blue.
Gray shapes sway as she moves.
Her dance an invitation. See it
and you sense her joy.

Conversation with White Rose

The cycle of winter
softens to spring. Your roots thicken and push down through
earth again, a dormancy becoming another birth.

It's morning, you and I are here with early feeders
next to a lake with silver carp and brown sunnies.
Carpenter bees, robins, grackles, a dove,
and great crow at her distance.

You and I, white rose, are anything but drowsy.
The sky's light turns your petals lavender blue
like a famous celebrity's eyes. I imagine you
in a raised garden, edged with trimmed grass
and women of different ages seated at a stone table
in metal chairs, having tea and serious conversation.

I remember a friend's mother I felt close to.
Her tender hands, velvet brown eyes. She wore your color
and wanted me to wear it instead of my black tee shirt.
Other roses surround us. Pinks, my favorite, and garnet red.
Amber Flush, a yellow. And tender lavender.

Today their necks lift skyward like yours.

Key West in January

Old Town Key West in January under stars, Mars the red planet and a sliver of new moon. Blue bougainvillea grows, thick-bushed, behind short fences. It clusters with white flowered shrubs next to wispy mimosa, its leaves like ferns. On Frances Street, alongside Key West Cemetery, elephant-ear-sized leaves stand out from thick green vines snugly surrounding magnolia, jacaranda and tall palm trees.

Green iguanas live between the headstones and rest in shaded tree branches. A kapok tree spreads its giant roots across the Light House lawn. Palms are wrapped in white and green tube lights every night a carnival. On Duval Street, sidewalk restaurant tables edged in tiny blue lights, stand next to coffee and gift shops, between tattoo salons, nail spas and bourbon bars. People walk the streets all day and all night.

Two macaws, one a fire engine red, the other blue-blue, preen and call, sitting on their long perches in the center of Duval Square. People bob their own heads, imitating the birds' movement. *Pretty boy, pretty boy, pretty girl.* They make clicking sounds and speak in singsong voices.

Bright-feathered wild chickens are everywhere. They sleep in trees. They strut and peck and crow all hours of the day and night. They scratch up tiny stones and sand from the brown ground. A clutch of young roosters has territory behind the porch we rent on Duval Street. Three gold-necked males face each other in a triangle almost every morning. They caw and clatter renewing their daily deals.

In ancient times, because cocks crowed with the rising sun, they were magic. Some thought they drove out ghosts and protected farm animals. Gypsy chickens with purple, green and gold feathers wear a king's cape. Locals still listen to chicken spirit, an incantation. Today chicken spirit calls. Speak up, speak up let them hear your voice, speak up, what are you waiting for?

Ode to Uncle Emory

Visiting you was like visiting the king of a tiny island
or someone from a country I had only read about.
The tallest man I've ever known, a man of the forest,
eyes like leaves.

For weeks, I'd anticipate our get-togethers, meeting you,
the magician of southern tracts and trails. You invited me
to explore the borders of cotton fields, creeks, and meadows,
divided by old oaks. We walked paths of yellow grass under
Spanish moss.

You taught me to notice how wind played at the tops of pines
and how to ask it what direction it came from. How to notice
who lived in tangled roots, the scent of pine and wild oleander,
which berries to eat and which berries to leave alone.

From your banjo, notes flowed out the window, out
the screen door, a greeting played to muted afternoons.
You taught me to see that planets don't twinkle. We'd stand,
looking up at Venus, present to the offerings of blue night.

Silent Auntie sat with her knitting, her knees crossed,
while we laced up our sneakers. Mehetabel the cat curled
into a spot of sun close to Auntie's feet, while Archie
was somewhere else, probably hiding in the kitchen.

One day while walking the trail, you said
if we were to be visited by aliens, they would come here
to out forest first before any other grove of trees. Amazed,
I held my breath and gazed at the sky with different eyes.

Under a Blue August Moon

a speculative vision

We think everyone inside is listening but not to me (or the three of thee with the still-life on the table in electric light). Turn it down and come on out to find me under a bright blue moon. Sky watchers are here. Come on! We have to meet them. The air is thin, it's limited. The woman from last night seriously told me that's how they do it when they're here, they're not always here. Sometimes disappearances happen. We didn't know.

Outside, a center scent of splinters is smoky. Inside the ceiling is dropped low, now with cracked paint. Come on through the hallway, darkened with the orange trumpet vines someone on the third floor wanted to cut all the way back. Cut out all the green. Listen, some are gathered at the second intersection. Now, I can't hear everything. Stop looking at me like that, I don't know any more than you do. According to CNN there have been no sightings of disappearances, yet, but that's the rumor. And the sky is cloudy. We have almost used our time.

Come on, come on, no more waiting. Stop fooling around. We talked about it. She told us the air is thin. This is serious. For centuries we knew it would happen. Our ancestors warned us to be ready. CNN now broadcast they are landing everywhere. They're carrying some kind of gear, boxes or blocks with tubes and wires, something like that. At the horizon, see the orange panorama? They look like us–but faster and smaller, they are four colors. It's going to take all of us. We knew they would come and we kept not learning, not learning anything. It's going to take all our resources, our children and grandchildren's children. We will need to want to join them. My Uncle Emory told me, remember what Harry Murphy said.

Come on—I don't want to go without you.

Three Hundred Poems

After all that came before, isolation
and a jealous stepfather, your mother, a mere girl,

was too young for parenting. Yet you were confident.
Under watching moons you explored miles

of railroad, desert and highway, carried your own
blessed heart out of muddy wetness

walked yellow fields hunted by hawks, grazed
by starlings. You rearranged your life on the northwest

coast at the water's edge. Slept in the narrow bed.
Kept cabinet doors closed. Learned three hundred poems

to save your own life and much later, at a microphone
shoulders squared over flat green earth

your voice sang out with an opening poem, a calling,
like a deep and heavy bell.

Standing Stones at Callanish

in the Outer Hebrides, Scotland

This must be another top to the world.
Twisting roads open out to a vista
that touches the entire sky.
Gray clouds swirl with the winds
over mica sand.
I come here to touch something
or something will touch me.
I've come to see the thirteen tall slabs
of silver rock that rest under
a full summer moon,

I've come to see the moon glide, as the stories say,
across the hills that look like a woman's body sleeping.
If you position yourself just right
the moon will roll for you along the hilltops
and come to center itself
above the standing stones at Callanish.
On the shortest night, the moon is still,
a sign from those who placed the stones.

I lean on the tallest. The light purifies me.
In that moment, they bless me, the wind whipping
through my hair. I am the wind,
my face against the purple sky.

Acknowledgments

Many thanks to the following publications and programs that have presented my work, sometimes in earlier versions:

Circumference: "Facts About the Body"

Connecticut River Review: "April's Good Neighbor," "Broad Winged Katydid Calls in September"

The Golden Thread: Connecting the Human Spirit Through the Arts: "Elegy for a Black Locust Tree"

Our Changing Environment (Guilford Poets' Guild)*:* "African Panorama"

Transitions and Transformations (Antrim House): "Animals Come", "Standing Stones at Callanish", "Volcano"

Where Flowers Bloom (Grayson Books): "Conversation with White Rose"

"Lady Slipper" poem with art by the poet, displayed on the grounds of Westmoor Park and Fernridge Parks in West Hartford, Connecticut for several years

Gratitude

My deepest thanks to friends and colleagues who have constantly supported me in my development as a poet. Thanks to The She's: Donna Fleisher, Marilyn Johnston, Rhett Watts, and Betti Viereck, for their friendship, sensitive insights, and encouragement. Thanks to the Partners in Poetry: Christine Beck, Ginny Connors, Debbie Gilbert, Pat Hale, Nancy Kerrigan, Julia Paul, and Elaine Zimmerman for their continued support over many years. Thanks to my dear friend Chris Sanders for being the first reader of this collection. Many thanks to Ginny Connors and Grayson Books for skill and encouragement in bringing this book to life. Heartfelt gratitude to Tom Nicotera for his continuous, outstanding support and occasional educationals on grammar and punctuation.

About the Author

Sherri (Sheryll) Bedingfield worked as a family therapist and psychotherapist for over 30 years. She used art and poetry with some of her clients. Bedingfield is the author of two previous poetry collections: *Transitions and Transformations* (Antrim House) and *The Clattering: Voices from Old Forfarshire, Scotland* (Grayson Books). Her work has appeared in *The Journal of Poetry Therapy* and many other journals and anthologies. Her poems have been performed by East Haddam Stage Company in their *Plays with Poetry* presentations. She has shared her poetry locally and in Dingle, Ireland. Bedingfield has served on the Board of the Riverwood Poetry Series in Hartford, Connecticut and has co-hosted the Wintonbury Poetry Series in Bloomfield, Connecticut. Bedingfield is on the Board of the Hartford Creative Contest, working with Hartford students to respond to prompts by writing essays, poetry, or by creating visual art.